Among the Lilies

Copyright © 2019 by Jane Heflin
All rights reserved

All Scripture quotations in this book, unless otherwise indicated, are taken from the New King James Version.
Copyright © 1982 by Thomas Nelson. Used by permission. All rights reserved.

Scripture quotations marked (NLT) are taken from the Holy Bible, New Living Translation, copyright ©1996, 2004, 2015 by Tyndale House Foundation. Used by permission of Tyndale House Publishers, Inc. Carol Stream, Illinois 60188. All rights reserved.

Scriptures marked NIV are taken from the NEW INTERNATIONAL VERSION (NIV): Scripture taken from THE HOLY BIBLE, NEW INTERNATIONAL VERSION ®. Copyright© 1973, 1978, 1984, 2011 by Biblica, Inc.™. Used by permission of Zondervan

Cover design by Joel Hosler

ISBN 9781098623708

Printed in the United States of America

To Ella Jane, Audra London, and August Sebastian Luke who are the future torch bearers of the gospel should the Lord tarry. Your childlike faith and innocence inspire me to live simply and love deeply. I love you with all of my heart.

Introduction

Among the Lilies is a collection of devotions, thoughts, poems, songs, and prayers that the Lord has shared with me as I continue on my journey of walking with Him.

Through the ups and the downs of life He has remained faithful to me. I grow to love Him more and more in my "beside the still waters" moments each day.

I started off this project for my family. I wanted to put the poems and songs I have written into one place to leave a part of me for the ones I hold near and dear to my heart. But as I began working on it I realized that it's possible that others might be blessed as well; thus, I compiled it into book form.

It truly is my prayer and desire that whoever reads the following pages will come to a deeper understanding of how much they are loved and that they would be inspired to be drawn into a deeper, more intimate relationship with the only One who loved them enough to die for their sin.

And for those who don't know Jesus as their Lord and Savior my prayer is that you will surely come to believe as you allow the Spirit of God to draw you into a personal relationship with Him as you read and think upon the following pages.

As I have received so I share with you that you also may believe.

To God be the glory, great things He has done!

Almighty God

"O LORD, our Lord, how excellent is Your name in all the earth,...when I consider Your heavens, the work of Your fingers, the moon and the stars, which You have ordained, what is man that You are mindful of him..." **Psalm 8:1, 3-4a**

Gazing out into the night sky my eyes are drawn to one particular very bright light glowing through millions of miles to reach my sight. I'm not sure whether it is a star or a planet but I watch to see where it is every night as I peer out my window. I stop to think about how we are in this vast universe floating on this amazing planet called Earth and how I am just one soul...like a tiny speck...among the billions of others living here - existing, moving, breathing - and yet - the Creator thinks upon me and loves me! I am filled with awe and wonder and my heart cries out:

Almighty God
Who am I
That You would set Your eyes on me
Eternal One
Redeeming Son
Became a man to set me free
I stand amazed in Your presence
You are worthy of praise
Almighty God
I'll worship You
For the rest of my days
You are love - You are God
You are good - You are holy
You are love - You are God
You are good - You are holy
Almighty God

Among the Lilies

"I am my beloved's, and my beloved is mine.
He feeds his flock among the lilies."
"Beautiful words stir my heart.
I will recite a lovely poem about the king,
for my tongue is like the pen of a skillful poet."
Song of Solomon 6:3
Psalm 45:1 NLT

Where does the Beloved feed His beloved?
The answer is found in Song of Solomon 6:3. It says among the lilies. Looking at verse 2 the Shulamite writes, **"My beloved has gone to his garden, to the beds of spices, to feed his flock in the gardens, and to gather lilies."**
Wow! What a beautiful picture of the perfect quiet place to meet with the lover of our soul - among a garden of lilies - like a secret garden secluded away where one may exclusively enter to meet with their Beloved!
In all actuality most of us don't have a garden of lilies to run to but we do have those special places that we can meet alone with our God where we can silence our souls and be still and listen for our Shepherd's voice.
If you haven't found that special place I sincerely suggest that you find one -- in your closet, on a bench at the park, a special room in your home, at the beach, or even your car! Think of that one place where you can escape for a while undisturbed. It's vital to our spiritual growth to hear what our Creator wants to say.
Just as our physical bodies need food to survive so our spiritual lives need to be fed from the Living Word of God. The Lover of our soul calls to us saying, "Rise up, my love, my fair one and come away."

Let us hear what our Lord has to say to us personally. He longs to give us peace and guidance every moment of every day.
May you find spiritual refreshment in your field of lilies.

Come speak to my heart
My Savior, God, and Friend
I've come to meet with You
In our quiet place once again
To our secret place - Where I seek Your face
Where Your mercies never end
In the garden of the lilies
My hungry soul is fed

You give me songs of praise
That rise within my soul
My lips shall speak of You
With the words of a poem
At Your feet I fall
It's Your voice I long to hear
Your whispers of love
As You bid me draw near

I will come to the garden
It's my source of delight
I will wait for You
All through the day and night
In the secret place - As I seek Your face
Just one look into Your eyes
In the garden of the lilies
My soul is satisfied
My soul is satisfied

You are Loved

"Then Christ will make His home in your hearts as you trust in Him. Your roots will grow down into God's love and keep you strong. And may you have the power to understand, as all God's people should, how wide, how long, how high, and how deep His love is. May you experience the love of Christ, though it is too great to understand fully. Then you will be made complete with all the fullness of life and power that comes from God." **Ephesians 3:17-19 NLT**

Oh, to truly know how much you are loved! We seek love from our parents, our spouse, our kids, our friends. They say they love us but as the saying goes, "Actions speak louder than words." The evidence of love sometimes is just not there through how we are spoken to or how we are treated. Since we are imperfect people living in a less than perfect world we truly are not capable of the unconditional love that only our God is able to give us. We just need to soak in that thought and realize the deep unfathomable fact that we have worth in His eyes and He - the God of this world - loves you intimately and unconditionally like no other. Think on this and believe it.

Through the eyes of God
You are beautiful
Through the eyes of God
You are loved
Through the eyes of God
You are a miracle
Fashioned by His hands
A work of art

You are loved - You are loved
By the God who made the earth and sea
If only you would just believe
You are loved - You are loved
By the God who sees each tear you cry
And every hurt you try to hide
You are loved

Through the eyes of God
You are royalty
Through the eyes of God
You're His child
Through the eyes of God
You are His precious one
Treasured by the Keeper of the stars

You are loved - You are loved
By the God who made the earth and sea
If only you would just believe
You are loved - You are loved
By the God who sees each tear you cry
And every hurt you try to hide
You are loved

You are loved - you are loved
Jesus came to die for you
God's only Son
No greater proof - that
You are loved - you are loved
Nothing you could ever do
Would keep your God from loving you
You are loved

For Such a Time as This

"Yet who knows whether you have come to the kingdom for such a time as this?" **Esther 4:14b**

All of us are here for a purpose whether we think so or not. We are all intricately woven in the whole scope of God's great plan. Some people are chosen by the Lord to be used in great ways to touch the lives of a vast number of people. Then there are many who somehow blend into the background feeling as if their lives count for little and that they could never possibly make a difference in this world. God calls us to live a life that is well-pleasing to Him -- a life of obedience -- and to be the example of Christ to a dying world. Like Queen Esther we may be placed in this life solely to speak at a certain moment in time which could impact the life of one person or many, such that they will be changed forever. Or you may be living in a household where your sphere of influence is with a spouse or your children while others may be called to the mission field to speak to the thousands or a few lives in a tiny village. Wherever or whenever -- it is for such a time as this. So what is our call? Simply obey.

God is always working even when I cannot see
He has a plan and purpose as He's watching over me
No life is wasted when placed into His hands
I need to be bold - I need to be strong - I need to stand

And if I should perish
I will perish
I must trust Him and obey
He'll never forsake me
For the kingdom is His
He's brought me to this place
For such a time as this

Nothing to fear now when God is in control
He knows the plans He has for me
He made my very soul
A life of full surrender when placed into His hands
Will help me be bold - will help me be strong - will help me to stand

Time is very precious
Not a moment now to waste
People all around me are dying without grace
Every life has meaning - A creation of God's hands
It's time to be bold - it's time to be strong - it's time to take a stand

And if I should perish
I will perish
I must trust Him and obey
He'll never forsake me
For the kingdom is His
He's brought me to this place
For such a time as this
He's brought me to this place
For such a time as this

Heart of a Servant

"'If I then, *your* Lord and Teacher, have washed your feet, you also ought to wash one another's feet. For I have given you an example, that you should do as I have done to you.'" John 13:14-15

Jesus, God in human flesh, stooped down and took on the role of a household servant to wash His disciples' feet including the smelly, dirty feet of His betrayer, Judas -- His enemy. Oh, for a heart like Jesus! We are such self-focused creatures living in a world that teaches that I am first. It's all about me - my feelings, my wants, my desires. "What about meeee???" But Jesus came and set the example of what true servanthood looks like. He, King of the universe, tells us to "wash one another's feet." In today's culture we don't usually go around offering to do that for one another but there are countless opportunities to do selfless acts of service. At home, on the job, at the mall - anywhere we find ourselves. The opportunities are all around us. Such as wiping that toddler's runny nose or changing that baby's stinky diaper or maybe it is merely doing your family's laundry or cooking dinner for someone in need. It could be as simple as picking up a piece of trash off the sidewalk or holding the door for someone. It's not about doing the bare minimum; it's about doing above and beyond. It's giving our best without reservation.

Lord, make this our prayer today:

Give me the heart of a servant
Make my life just like Your Son's
Let others see Your beauty in me
A reflection of Your perfect love
I don't desire greatness
Nor fame of any kind

I just want to be in Your perfect will
Serving You with heart, soul, and mind
Give me the heart of a servant
Make my life just like Your Son's
Let others see Your beauty in me
A reflection of Your perfect love
A reflection of Your perfect love

One selfless act of obedience
Leaving the splendor from on high
To come and live upon this earth
And give His life for mine
The cross He bore - the price He paid
His sacrifice of love
No other will ever compare
To Jesus my beloved

Endure Good Soldier

As a Christ-follower we are all leaders in one way or another, whether it's in the home as the overseer of the little "lambs" God has blessed you with or at your place of employment. You may be the boss of your department or the supervisor of your shift. Maybe your calling of leadership is in the church as a ministry head or of a group. Wherever the Lord has placed us we all need to be encouraged to endure and forge forward as a good soldier in the army of the Lord. It's been a blessing to sit under some wonderful teachers of the word and many have been an inspiration to keep the faith and to carry on. If you should find yourself in a place of discouragement or defeat in this role as a leader take the following to heart and allow the Lord to use your life as an example for others to model.

Endure good soldier keep the faith
The battle has been won
The Mighty God of Israel
Through Jesus Christ His Son
Has gained the victory at the cross
We fight in His great name
Though Satan's army rages on
His battle is in vain
I've watched you on the battlefield
Your life has been hit hard
Your faith in Christ has never failed
Though wounded you've carried on
And when you're called to lead your troops
You encounter the enemy first
Yet you don't retreat and wave your flag
You carry on even though it hurts

Dear leader of your precious flock
Your example of God's love
Has touched the heart of many
You're a blessing from above
So, carry on good soldier of the faith
Press on in Jesus' name
The war will soon be over
And with Jesus we shall reign

One small vessel to be poured into
One little light to shine
One voice crying in the darkness
What little I have is Thine
Take this life - it's Yours not mine
What little there is may You multiply
For I am Yours today - now and forever
No turning back - there is no other way
I am Yours - You are mine
I will proclaim and lift high
The Name above all names
The Name of Jesus
Jesus

Truly Blessed

God has truly blessed me!
I was born into a wonderful, loving family. Dad worked hard and provided for his family. He was a quiet man and even though he worked a full time job and worked a side job on Saturdays he was still there to help my mom when he was home. My mom was a gentle soul and lovingly took care of her children. We grew up with little but Dad and Mom provided the security of a peaceful and loving environment... something I will be eternally grateful for.
Growing up as the middle child and only girl had its advantages but sometimes it would have been nice to have had a sister. Didn't really think about it when I was young but when I got married and had two daughters I realized how much the Lord loved me when He blessed us with girls. I was always mom first and foremost. Being a Christ-follower I realized the importance of nurturing them in the ways of the Lord but as they grew they became my sisters and friends. Heart of my heart - truly I am blessed!

I gaze upon a picture of my beautiful girls and me
My mind travels to years ago and the treasured memories
It seems it was only yesterday that I held them in my arms
Their chubby cheeks and innocent little faces their sweetness and their charm
It was my heart's desire to raise them in the Lord
I trusted and I prayed and sought God's holy word
Each unique and special with talents from God above
He blessed them with amazing gifts that evidenced His love
They grew in grace and beauty with hearts of purity
The blessings now I reap with joy for it's now come back to me

Every moment I spend with my girls is a treasure that never ends
For they are not just my daughters but my sisters and my friends
Engraved forever in the recesses of my heart into eternity
Thank You, Lord, for the blessing of Audra and Tiffany

Take Heart

Take heart - don't despair - be encouraged
For the Lord your God is in control
The Maker of the moon and stars
Keeps watch over your very soul
He upholds the earth with His strong hand
And His eye is on the weak
He knows your thoughts - the deepest part
And is aware of your every need
Cast every care upon Him now
He's right there by your side
Lift up your voice and seek His face
He longs to bless your life
Surely His goodness and mercy and grace have no bounds
Amazing is the love of Christ
So take heart - don't despair - be encouraged
In His presence forever abide

I Am

"Jesus said to them, 'Most assuredly, I say to you, before Abraham was, I AM.'" John 8:58

What is your need at this moment?
Are you in a state of depression feeling as if a big black cloud is over your head and there is no chance of the sun breaking through any time soon? Maybe you are in an abusive relationship whether it is physical, verbal, or emotional and you can't go on any more like this. Maybe you have slipped into a place of sin that you never thought you would go and you feel as if God will just not be able to forgive you this time. Could it be that you have lost your loved one and don't know how you are going to be able to go on without them. Perhaps you are very ill and the doctors have nothing more they can do for you or maybe your husband just left you for someone younger and prettier leaving you with absolutely nothing. Whatever place you are in - whatever situation you find yourself - there is **nothing** too difficult or impossible for God. He is the "I AM" for you now - and always. The Lord whispered these words of love to me and I share them with you.

I am the God that healeth thee
I am the God who sets you free
I am the Keeper of your soul
I am the One Who makes you whole
I am the Bread of Life for you
I will make your heart brand new
I am the bright and morning star
I am the Shepherd of your heart
I am your God - I am your King
I am everything you'll ever need
I am God
I am the Lamb the final sacrifice
Took all the blame as I gave My life

I am the Son of God Most High
I am Emmanuel - Jesus Christ
I am your God - I am your King
I am everything you'll ever need
I am God

Still a Work in Progress

I'm still a work in progress, Lord
Even though I'm further down the road
I've walked the path for several years
And still have a long way to go
How grateful I am for Your mercy
Your holy word I treasure more than gold
Your promises are sure and guide my steps
To lead me all the way home
Refine me - revive me - help me not to lose heart
For at times this journey is steep
And the way gets dark
Yet I know You are faithful - Your everlasting arms are strong
Lifting me up when I am weak
Giving me strength to carry on
Lord, You are my firm foundation
My life is built on You Jesus, my King
There's no greater love I have ever known
No one else gives me reason to sing
I will keep trusting and praying and seeking Your face
For You're the answer to my every heart's cry
I will pick up the cross that You've fashioned for me
As You make me broken bread and poured out wine

The Surprise of My Life

Having only girls my husband would frequently express the desire to have a son. But the thought of another child when my youngest was 12 -- not to mention my not so fond memories of morning sickness for almost 5 months during my prior pregnancies -- was just not a joyful suggestion.
Um, no, I don't think so! Besides, life was good. We were apartment managers where we lived in an old small house which helped reduce our rent. We were homeschooling and involved with various ministries at church. The girls were older and more independent. But flu-like symptoms had come upon me - fatigue, nausea, loss of appetite. My sister-in-law who worked for our doctor suggested I get checked out... perhaps get a pregnancy test!!!! The phone call came and sure enough -- I was PREGNANT!
Dear God, how could this be true? I am 35! Too old to have another child! But as I was to learn, God is **always** in control. Yes, I had morning sickness but I made it through. Yes, I was starting all over again - in a sense - but I wouldn't change it now for the world. And yes, I made it through the labor and delivery experience one more time and gave birth to a healthy beautiful baby boy with blue eyes. He brought joy and laughter to our small family and he had older sisters to dote on him and they were a great help to me.
Nathanael Steven Paul when translated means: "little crowned gift from God." And that is what he remains to be until this day -- though not so little anymore. He is a gentleman with a compassionate, caring heart. He has a calm and quiet God-fearing spirit.
When the Lord brought our boy into our lives I realized in a deeper way just how much God loves us and desires to bless us.

I wasn't asking for more children at the time but God heard the desires of my husband's heart and through it He blessed us all. I think of James 1:17, ***"Every good gift and every perfect gift is from above, and comes down from the Father of lights, with whom there is no variation or shadow of turning."***

Father knows best
He knows what He's doing
Even down to the slightest detail
He has a plan and we must trust Him
For His promises never fail
Leave it all in the Savior's keeping
Take one moment at a time
He never slumbers
He's never too early
Never ahead and never behind
We're the clay on the wheel He is spinning
The Master Potter is mindful of you and me
As He patiently molds with great love and delight
Our lives into vessels of beauty

All of You

"'He must increase, but I must decrease.'" John 3:30

No one said this journey through life would be stress-free. Having been born into a world full of sin definitely doesn't make it any easier. It doesn't matter what kind of upbringing we have either. We could have had it tough growing up where nothing came easy or we could have been born with a silver spoon in our mouths. We could have had great parents, lousy parents, one parent, or no parent. But we are all without excuse when we get older having reached the age of accountability when we know right from wrong. For there are only two ways to go - my way or God's - accept Christ or reject Him. Once we choose life by accepting Christ some say that life gets easier. We must remember though that we are still living in this fallen world and we still have to deal with the "old me" - and - we still live among all the other fellow sinners we come in contact with on a daily basis. But God didn't leave us on our own. We have our greatest example before us. Jesus paved the path for us - all the way to the cross. We just need to begin to follow His blood-stained footsteps. The Savior's time on earth was not a walk in the park and neither will ours be. The old nature needs to be buried and rendered dead and the new nature must be nurtured in God's word and love. Every moment of every day is a new chance to surrender. Surrender what? Everything that is not pleasing to the Lord. It's more and more of Jesus and a lot less of me. This will not happen overnight. It is a lifelong process.

All of You - none of me
So when others see me
They see You
Beautiful, lovely, altogether true
That's when it's none of me and all of You

Though the process may not be easy
Painful at times it will be
Make me a masterpiece for Your kingdom
So all the world can see
That it's all of You and none of me

The Truest of Loves

I am obsessed with Jesus
He is the passion of my life
I am in love with my Savior
He is my Husband - I am His bride
He is perfect and oh, so holy
He is more beautiful by far
His love for me is unfailing
He holds every beat of my heart

I Will See You Through

We have all experienced those times at one point or another in our lives when we reach the end of our rope and we are screaming inside ourselves with things like: "That's it, I can't take anymore!" "I can't go on like this!" "This hurts too much!" "When will this trial end?" "When will you take care of this for me, Lord?" You pray, you cry, you seek counsel. You fast and plead before the Lord. There is no immediate answer and you wonder if God is listening. And then when you think things couldn't get any worse than they are something even more devastating happens. In Luke 11:9-10 as Jesus was teaching His disciples about prayer He told them, "And so I tell you, keep on asking, and you will receive what you ask for. Keep on seeking, and you will find. Keep on knocking, and the door will be opened to you. For everyone who asks, receives. Everyone who seeks, finds. And to everyone who knocks, the door will be opened."(NLT) We must not lose heart! We must keep on praying, asking, seeking, knocking, and trusting. Jesus will bring the answer in His timing and whatever that answer is it will be what's best for us in our particular circumstance. Whatever He brings to us He will see us through. That's a promise. And so it was that during a time of deep despair the Lord spoke the following to me...

I will see you through
I will see you through
There is nothing, My child
That I cannot do
Take hold of My hand
I am faithful and true
And if you can't walk
I will carry you
I was with My Son
Until the end

Never faltered or failed
You see, My friend
He walked the road
You are taking now
He made it through
So will you, My child
I will see you through
I will see you through
There is nothing, My child
That I cannot do
Take hold of My hand
I am faithful and true
And if you can't walk
I will carry you
And if you can't walk
I will carry you

Someday we'll have all the answers
To the vexing questions of life
The things that man tries to search out
Consumed daily in emptiness and strife
If we were to know as our Creator knows all
Then He would reveal it as plain as the day
But He is God and we are but dust
We just need to trust Him and obey

This Mother's Prayer

***"...Sit still, my daughter, until you know how the matter will turn out..."* Ruth 3:18**

Oh, the sweet trials of raising children! I can call it "sweet" because all of mine are grown and I know each stage of their lives caused me to learn many valuable lessons. I can now look back with a smile and thank God for seeing me through. Each step in the journey has its moments such as when they are little and they require a lot of patience, care, time, and energy. As they become more independent the testing doesn't end but prayers of wisdom are needed to make godly decisions -- especially with the first child. With the firstborn it's trial and error as they are like our little experiment to learn from for the next child of what worked and what didn't. And as they grow into young adulthood and they don't seem to be following the path you thought they should be then you need to let go and trust that God brought them into this world and He is more than capable of guiding them in the right direction... such as it was for me. I had left home when I turned 18 and moved across the country. I didn't consider how my mother felt as she cried as I left. I was only thinking of **me** and what **I** wanted.

And now here I was years later with my daughter -- my "baby" -- leaving to do **her** thing not thinking about anyone but **herself** -- off to do what **she** wanted with no consideration of **my** feelings and what **I** thought she should be doing --and it hit me in the face as I heard the Lord saying to me, "Jane, you are now experiencing the same heartache that your mother endured over 20 years ago and I believe you owe her an apology." I did apologize but it didn't help my own personal pain at that moment to go away.

The Lord was so very dear and close to me during that season of my life.

He showed me that He would make everything beautiful in His time and give beauty for ashes and joy instead of mourning. And you know what? He did!
Don't give up! Keep on praying for that son or daughter. God is faithful!

Do I love her enough to let her go
Do I trust You enough to say "Yes"
Even though the pain remains in my heart
I'm confident that Father knows best
I know in time You will heal every wound
And wipe away every tear from my face
Yet the scars will remain to always remind me
Of Your wonderful, beautiful grace
In Your eyes she's a work in progress
Clay on Your Potter's wheel
As You mold and You shape and perhaps even break
The result will bring forth Your perfect will
Lord, as for myself I've been stubborn and hard-headed
I traveled down a dark, sinful path
Yet You found me, called me, made me brand new
And saved me from destruction and wrath
Help me remember that as You saw me through
And had a plan for my life
You'll do the same for my daughter, too
For You are Lord, You are King, You are Christ
Oh, Jesus, hear this prayer tonight
This mother's heart cries out to You
You have traveled down this road before
I know You will see me through

The Lord Is near to the Brokenhearted

The older we get the more we witness the passing away of others. When someone leaves this earth as a believer it is a glorious thing but those who are left behind experience great loss in losing that someone near and dear to them. Jesus understands our pain of loss as we see in John 11 with the story of Lazarus whom Jesus loved. Lazarus had already been in the grave for 4 days before Jesus arrived on the scene. As He saw all the people weeping and mourning as He went to where they had buried Lazarus John writes in verse 35 that Jesus wept. Jesus' heart was broken to see what the result of sin had brought forth. God had originally created a perfect world where mankind would have never died...that is until man sinned and since then physical death is inevitable for all His creation. But thanks be to God for Jesus who conquered death and the grave as He paid for our sins at the cross of Calvary. As He told Martha, Lazarus's sister, **"I am the resurrection and the life. He who believes in Me, though he may die, he shall live. And whoever lives and believes in Me shall never die. Do you believe this?"**

Because He lives we shall live. Do you as a Christ-follower believe this? We have hope! This life is not the end. We shall see all those who have gone on before us who accepted Jesus as their Savior. They are beholding the face of the Lord and soon we will be there, too. Oh, happy day!!! May the following words bring you comfort if you find yourself in that place of mourning and loss.

The Lord is near to the brokenhearted
He longs to hold you close
And wipe your eyes
Each tear you've cried
And bring comfort to your soul

Fall into the arms of Jesus
Find refuge in the shelter of His wings
He knows your thoughts
The deepest part
You don't have to say a thing

He understands the pain of loss
The hurt, the sorrow, the grief
As the days go by
In His presence abide
He alone can give you peace

Allow the Shepherd to lead you
To lie down in meadows of green
To bask in the love
From the Father above
Beside His quiet streams

Dear precious one of the living God
Know that I'm praying for you
My heart is aching
It truly is breaking
In this season you're going through

Keep your eyes fixed on your Savior
He will be your guide until the end
And one day soon
We will be there, too
United with family and friends

Oh, for that day when we see Jesus
When we shall see Him face to face
No more suffering or pain
The former things will fade away
In the light of His glory and grace

Let Not Your Heart Be Troubled

When the call came into the church office about a fellow sister in the Lord who tragically lost her daughter in a car accident it was the news no one ever expects or desires to hear. No words can be expressed at that moment. The only comforting thought was that the young girl was in the presence of the Lord. As I thought about her there in heaven and what she was possibly experiencing the following words came to my heart as an expression of what one might want to convey to loved ones left here mourning their loss.

Let not your heart be troubled
Nor let it be afraid
I'm at home in Heaven
In the throne room of His grace
Where the angels gather round
In His presence I am found
It's more beautiful than words could ever say

Weep no more for me
For I have been set free
In the arms of Jesus I am safe
No more crying here
No more pain or fear
In the arms of Jesus I am safe

Let not your heart be troubled
Nor let it be afraid
There are many mansions
He's prepared for me this place
And if you will just believe
Open your heart and just receive
Then we'll never have to say goodbye again

Weep no more for me
For I have been set free
In the arms of Jesus I am safe
No more crying here
No more pain or fear
In the arms of Jesus I am safe
In the arms of Jesus I am safe

Our Great Shepherd

I shall not want when the Lord is my Shepherd
He loves me and leads me beside the peaceful streams
He restores my soul when I am worn and tired
He gives me my heart's desires and fulfills all my dreams
He carries me when I can walk no further
When I am weak He is strong
When danger arises I need not fear
For I know in Whom I belong
And if I should stray - His watchful eye is on me
He will leave the flock to bring me home
My Shepherd is my Protector and He loves me
In Him I am never alone

Good Night Sweet Angel of God
In Memory of Crystal

"But Jesus said, 'Let the little children come to Me, and do not forbid them; for of such is the kingdom of heaven.'" **Matthew 19:14**

Good night sweet angel of God
I know we will see you again
Everyone will miss you
You've touched each of our lives
All of your family and friends
Good night sweet angel of God
I know we will see you again
You left the world behind
When you closed your tired eyes
And awoke into a place that has no end
Your life held such a witness
You left an imprint on our lives
In the short time that we knew you
We were blessed with your faith in Christ

Good night sweet angel - rest peacefully with Jesus
Cradled in His arms of love
Every tear you've ever cried
He's wiped away from your eyes
You'll never have to hurt again
Into His holy presence
You're there before His throne
Beholding now the face of God
You are home

Soldiers of Christ Put on Your Armor

Soldiers of Christ put on your armor
Arise to the battle
The victory is sure
Forward we march with confidence and courage
The battle was won on Calvary's hill

The enemy may roar like a lion
But a liar and deceiver is he
This foe has been conquered
We shall not fear
Our debt has been paid
We are free

Oh, to have a heart like Jesus
To imitate the Apostle Paul
Willing to lay our life down completely
Willing to give our very all
Make us, break us, empty us, dear Lord
Till everything is gone
Fill us with Your Holy Spirit
Give us the grace to carry on

You Are the Lamb

" Behold! The Lamb of God who takes away the sin of the world!" **John 1:29**

Our world is filled with so many "gods" and so many say that many roads lead to Heaven. How can we know which one is true? Which one is right?
John 3:16 tells us that God the **Creator** loved the world He **created** so much that He gave His only Son to die for all mankind. No other "god" ever came down in human flesh to live a sinless life among His creation and then gave His perfect life for all who would believe except Jesus Christ. He became the sacrificial Lamb who shed His blood for our sin so we could be made right with God. It's as simple to believe as this - Jesus came from Heaven to earth to the cross to the grave and back to Heaven all because of His amazing grace and love for us.

You are the Lamb who died for me
You shed Your blood to wash me clean
Surrendered Your will so that I could be
A child of the Father throughout eternity
You are the Lamb - God's precious Lamb
Willing to die for me
You are the Lamb - the spotless Lamb
God's sacrifice - You gave Your life
You are the Lamb
And if I was the only one
In the world I do believe
You would have come to earth
And died just for me
You are the Lamb - God's precious Lamb
Willing to die for me
You are the Lamb - the spotless Lamb
God's sacrifice - You gave Your life
You are the Lamb

See What He's Done

No fault could be found in Jesus my Lord
Yet they chose to crucify the One I adore
They mocked and beat the Great I AM
No beauty found in God's precious Lamb
What have they done?

Look what we've done
To God's only Son
Despised and rejected
By everyone
Humbled in silence
Not a word did He speak
This spotless Lamb - so gentle and meek

See what He's done
Came from all eternity
Left His home in glory
All because of His love
For you and me

Jesus Has Risen

Early in the morning before the dawn of the day
The women brought spices to the tomb where Christ lay
But when they arrived they found the stone rolled away
Looking in - they heard an angel proclaim

Jesus has risen - He's not here - He has risen
Jesus has risen - He's not here - He has risen from the dead

With fear and great joy the women fled from the tomb
They found the disciples and delivered the news
Some chose to doubt even though Christ had said,
"On the third day I will rise from the dead"

Jesus has risen - He's not here - He has risen
Jesus has risen - He's not here - He has risen from the dead

Christ did appear in the midst of His friends
He spoke words of peace that He'd come back again
He promised His Spirit to those who would wait
He rose up to Heaven as the angels proclaimed

Jesus has risen - He's not here - He has risen
Jesus has risen - He's not here - He has risen from the dead
Just as He said
Just as He said

What Wondrous Love Can This Be

What wondrous love can this be
That You would come here to me
I see the love within Your eyes
Your arms stretched wide for me
The scars that speak of sacrifice
You gave it all with Your own life
Yet doubt and fear still cloud my view
Of drawing near to You

Oh help me, dear Jesus, and make my life new
Here on my knees I bow to You
Free me from all of the pain deep within
And cleanse me from all of my sin

What wondrous love can this be
That You would come here to me
You've opened up my eyes to see
And Jesus now I believe - I believe - I believe

You Are the Rock of Ages

You are the Rock of Ages
A shelter from the storm
And under Your wings I'll take refuge
Upon You I will call

I will cry to You in trouble
I'll praise You in times of peace
In Your loving arms I'll tarry
There's no place I'd rather be

You are the Rock of Ages
A shelter from the storm
And under Your wings I'll take refuge
Upon You I will call

You have heard me in times of trouble
Your mercy and love never cease
In Your presence I'll dwell forever
There's no place I'd rather be

You are the Rock of Ages
A shelter from the storm
And under Your wings I'll take refuge
Upon You I will call
Upon You I will call
Upon You I will call

Thank You, Lord

Thank You, Lord, for loving me
Your grace and mercy undeserved
Yet I am free
Lead me on day by day
Precious Lord, guide my way
In my weakness make me strong
I know You're with me though the journey is long
Days of heartache - days of pain
Yet You are with me still the same
Yet You are with me still the same
Jesus - Rock of Ages
A shelter from the storms of life
Everlasting arms of comfort
Keep me safe through the night
Gentle Healer - Holy Father
Mighty God - Lord of all
Humbled in Your holy presence
At Your feet I will bow

Today's the Day

Nowhere else to turn
No other place to hide
Can't run away anymore
Time to stop and look inside

Harden not your heart
Open up your mind
Listen to this plea
So you won't be left behind

Today's the day - today's the day
His love is reaching out to you
Don't turn and walk away
Today's the day - today's the day
His love is reaching out to you
Don't turn and walk away

No one understands
It seems like no one cares
You're feeling all alone
As if there's no one there

There's One who hears your cries
Who's feeling all your pain
He takes you as you are
His love will never change

Today's the day - today's the day
His love is reaching out to you
Don't turn and walk away
Today's the day - today's the day
His love is reaching out to you
Don't turn and walk away

No matter where've you been or what you've done
You can find forgiveness in the love of His Son

Today's the day - today's the day
His love is reaching out to you
Don't turn and walk away
Today's the day - today's the day
His love is reaching out to you
Don't turn and walk away

Today's the day

Make Me a Friend like You

***"Greater love has no one than this, than to lay down one's life for his friends."* John 15:13**

My Dad said something to me when I was in my teens that I have never forgotten through the years. On the subject of having friends he told me, "I can count my friends on my one hand." I thought to myself at the time, "Oh, poor Dad. That's it? I have tons of friends."
As the years have passed and I matured in my walk with the Lord I came to realize this was true for me, too.
So many people come in and out of our lives. Very few are deemed a "true" friend… that someone who can be counted on to be there for you. To pray for you, encourage you, to speak truth when you've veered off course and to speak words of wisdom and perhaps lay down their life for you. Solomon understood this as he shared in Proverbs 20:6,
"Many will say they are loyal friends, but who can find one who is truly reliable?" NLT
Because we are all imperfect people we will fail each other at times. But Jesus, our forever Friend, will never fail us. He is constant and will be faithful to the end of time.
Dear Lord, may I be a better friend as I follow Your example. Make me a friend like You.

I have found a friend in You
What a perfect friend You are
You meet my every need, oh God
You heal my broken heart
You lift me up when I am down
You are faithful and true
Lord, make me a friend like You

Love through me
Live through me

May I be Your hands and feet
To the lost and lonely sinner
Please give me eyes to see
May I wipe those tears
Of a hurting soul
May I listen carefully
May I pray for the needs of others
Before I think of me
Lord, make me a friend like You

I have found a friend in You
What a perfect friend You are
Your wondrous love washes over me
You keep no record of my wrongs
You died for me when I wasn't Your friend
For You are faithful and true
Lord, make me a friend like You

Love through me
Live through me
May I be Your hands and feet
To the lost and lonely sinner
Please give me eyes to see
May I wipe those tears
Of a hurting soul
May I listen carefully
May I pray for the needs of others
Before I think of me
Lord, make me a friend like You

Greater love has no one than this
Than to lay down one's life for his friends
Lord, make me a friend like You
Lord, please make me a friend like You

He Is Watching over You

"The eyes of the LORD are on the righteous, and His ears are open to their cry…the righteous cry out, and the LORD hears, and delivers them out of all their troubles." **Psalm 34:15, 17**

Take your problems to God
Just give Him your every hurt
And trust Him
Jesus is right by your side
He'll comfort your aching heart
Just ask Him - ask Him
He is watching over you
He knows what you're going through
He is watching over you
He knows what you're going through
Keep your eyes on Him
He is watching over you
Through the valleys He'll be there
He'll never forsake His own
He loves you
Jesus gave His life for you
There's nothing that He can't do
Believe Him - He loves you
He is watching over you
He knows what you're going through
He is watching over you
He knows what you're going through
Keep your eyes on Him
He is watching over you
Keep your eyes on Him
He is watching over you

Oh, Child of God

Oh, child of God, please hear His voice
He's calling out to you
To leave the world behind you
And do as He would do
To be holy as He is holy
Hate the things that will bring you harm
The devil will entice you
With his scheming and his charm
He throws his bait to simple ones
He'll deceive you and he'll steal
He'll give you anything you want
Then reel you in for the merciless kill
Oh, child of God, don't let him prey
Upon your weakened soul
Draw close to God and seek His will
Make sure you truly know
That walking closely every day
With the One who died for you
Is the only way that brings joy and peace
The only way that is true
Oh, child of God, please listen
Be separate from the world today
Walk in the light of His glorious presence
For Jesus is the only way

My Soul Safely Rests

My soul safely rests in the arms of my Father
Where I find peace and fullness of joy
By the still streams of mercy I linger
Seeking His face and longing for His voice

And I rest - my soul rests - safely in the arms of the
One who knows best
All through the day and into the night
My soul safely rests in the arms of Christ

Amidst the chaos and trials of this life
In the middle of the storms, confusion and strife
He is my anchor and He is my guide
I safely rest - my soul satisfied

And I rest - my soul rests - safely in the arms of the
One who knows best
All through the day and into the night
My soul safely rests in the arms of Christ

Nothing comes my way that He's not allowed
Every season of life can be met with a smile
For He is my comfort - on Christ's rock I stand
My soul safely rests in the mercy of His plan

And I rest - my soul rests - safely in the arms of the
One who knows best
All through the day and into the night
My soul safely rests in the arms of Christ

He leads me to rise up and come away
There I will meet Him in our quiet place
He sings over me with His song from above
I melt in His presence and bask in His love

And I rest - my soul rests - safely in the arms of the
One who knows best
All through the day and into the night
My soul safely rests in the arms of Christ
All through the day and into the night
My soul safely rests in the arms of Christ

Soldiers of the Army of God

Soldiers of the army of God
Rise up to the call today
Do not fear - the victory is won
For our Commander-in-Chief leads the way
He knows the strategies of the enemy
And He will train our hands for war
So rise up to the call, good soldiers
For the battle is the Lord's

For we walk by faith and not by sight
Taking one step at a time
If God is for us who can be against us
Leave the world behind
And take one day at a time

Smile upon Your Daughter

Smile upon Your daughter
Enfold her in Your arms
Fill her with Your Spirit
Keep her from all harm
May she always sense Your presence
Dear Jesus, to You I pray
May You grant her the desires You've placed in her heart
Through open doors along life's way
You are her God and Father
The lover of her soul
May you bless her with Your goodness
May Your Spirit be in control
May she find favor in Your sight
Precious Lord and Mighty King
Pour out Your blessings on Your beloved
May You be her everything
Thank You for this special child
Your princess, my sister and friend
I bring my daughter before Your throne
Where Your mercies never end

Make Your Presence Known

Jesus, sweet Jesus
Make Your presence known here
In this holy place
Jesus, sweet Jesus
As You walk amongst us
Beholding every face
Fill us with Your power
Melt our hearts this very hour
Teach us, heal us
Make us one
Let Your will be done
Fill us with Your power
Melt our hearts this very hour
Bring us to our knees
That we may worship Thee

I want to lose myself in You, my Savior
I want to please You and obey Your every word
May I let go of my pride and all that is inside
May I be empty of myself - yes, crucified
May every word - every thought - be pleasing to You, Lord
May I put others' needs before my own
May I do just as You say
As I serve You day to day
May I be a living sacrifice - yes, full of praise

Rabboni

Luke tells the story of 2 sisters named Mary and Martha. They along with their brother Lazarus loved Jesus. Jesus loved them and spent time at their home.

Martha was one who loved to serve and on one of His visits as Jesus entered their village it was Martha who welcomed Jesus into her house. Luke shares that Martha was distracted with much serving as she was probably preparing a meal for her Guest and possibly the disciples who were traveling with Jesus. As Jesus was teaching I'm sure Martha was listening as she ran about getting things in order but Mary was found sitting at His feet listening to what He taught. When Martha came to her Friend, Jesus, she complained about Mary's lack of assistance in helping her do the work and felt He should tell Mary to help her.

Jesus told Martha that there was one thing needed and that her sister Mary had discovered it. Martha was distracted while Mary was focused. In modern day talk I guess you could say Martha was multi-tasking.

Someone once shared that there is no truth to multi-tasking for our attention is divided and one of the things we are trying to do will suffer. Research shows that our brains can only focus on one thing at a time and when we try to do two things at once, our brain lacks the capacity to perform both tasks successfully.

Jesus knew that all along. After all, **He** designed the brain!

As Martha worried and was upset over all the details Mary was commended for discovering the only one thing worth being concerned about and that would not be taken away from her.

In Matthew 26:7, Mark 14:3, John 11:2 and 12:1-8, we find that Mary anointed the Lord with costly fragrant oil and wiped His feet with her hair. Mary worshipped her Lord extravagantly and made it a priority over all the serving and fluff to sit at His feet and listen to His voice. She did not let anything or anyone intrude into her times of worship of her first love.

Time spent in prayer, worship, and listening to the voice of Jesus is time wisely spent and never a waste.

In examining ourselves one might ask, "How am I spending my time?" There are so many things to distract us as we go throughout our day such as electronics and gadgets and the infatuation of social media consuming our precious time.

The Spirit of the living God is calling. Jesus, the One Mary Magdalene called "Rabboni", is calling. He is calling me and He is calling you.

> *When was the last time that you sat at Jesus' feet*
> *And sang Him praise songs so sweet*
> *Jesus is waiting for me and for you*
> *He desires sweet fellowship, too*
> *Learn from the Master*
> *Dine with the Lord*
> *Great are His promises*
> *Rich are His rewards*
> *Gaze upon His holiness*
> *Look deep into His eyes*
> *Feed upon His faithfulness*
> *His love you can't deny*
> *His love for you*
> *His love for me*
> *Rabboni*
> *Master Rabboni*
> *Rabboni - Can you call Him your Master Rabboni*

Do you really know my Jesus
Do you really know His love
Do you truly want to be with Him
And listen to His voice
Do you soar with Him to higher heights
Do you draw close and feel His heart
Do you dance with Him in the valley
And embrace Him in the dark
Is He on your mind throughout the day
In the morning when you arise
At night when the day is done and before you close your eyes
Do you trust Him as you fall asleep
As you whisper your words of love
That He would watch you and keep you in His care
As He will - He does

God's Love Letter

I live upon Your word, oh God
It is my daily bread
Every word You speak is pure and true
To give warning for what lies ahead
Your word brings comfort to my soul
In my weakness it makes me strong
It's a light that overcomes the darkness
And reveals when I am wrong
Your word is sweeter than honey
Yet it's sharper than any two-edged sword
It's living and powerful - exposing my thoughts
Piercing deeply into the innermost core
Your word will stand forever, Lord
It gives me counsel and is my delight
It burns within me like a fire
And is my meditation day and night
I will hide Your word within my heart
That I might not sin against You
For it will keep me on the narrow path
Guiding me all the way through
As Your word goes forth and will not return void
But will accomplish what You please
It will prosper everywhere that You send it
Producing the fruit of joy and peace
Your word is like hidden treasure
If I take the time to seek and find
Great and precious are Your promises
I can claim them all as mine
You left us with Your very word
Given for a world in need
This love letter from Your very heart
May we open it and receive

Lord, How I Long for Your Presence

Lord, how I long for Your presence
Lord, how I long for Your touch
Just one glimpse into Your eyes, sweet Jesus
How I desire to be with You so much
You hold my heart - You hold my hand
How I delight to follow Your command
Closer and closer and closer to Thee
This is the only place I want to be
You are my morning - You are my night
All through the day in darkness and light
Draw me nearer, precious Jesus
To rise up and come away
You are my Beloved
Draw me nearer this very day
You are my Prince
My love, my life
You are my Husband
I am Your bride
Just You and I
As one we will be
Together forever
Throughout eternity
I love You, my Jesus, my Lord, my God
In our secret place stay with me
In my heart
You will always be

It must be complete surrender
For the Father to have His way in me
So I may be more like Jesus
For all the world to see
His kindness, His beauty, His splendor
The aroma of life - His love
Sweet Spirit of the living God
Fall fresh from heaven above
May it be, Lord
All about You
Every word, every thought
Every motive of my heart
May it be - let it be
All about You

Lift up Your Head

Lift up your head
Lift up your voice
For our God reigns over the earth
Mercy and truth
Unfailing love
Open your eyes and see that God is good!
He never fails or falters
His love forever endures
Break out in songs of joy
For He is good
As the sun that shines
His promises are sure
Cast away your fear and doubt
And claim what's yours
And claim what's yours in Christ

Follow Me

Jesus told His followers that the Spirit alone gives eternal life while human effort accomplishes nothing. He told them that the very words He speaks are spirit and life. But some did not believe and many walked away and followed Him no more. Jesus then asked His 12 disciples if they were going to leave and Peter said, **"Lord, to whom would we go? You have the words that give eternal life. We believe and we know You are the Holy One of God."** John 6:68-69 NLT

On another occasion Jesus asked His disciples, **"Who do men say I, the Son of Man, am?"** And they answered that some were saying Elijah or John the Baptist, Jeremiah or one of the prophets…..

Then the pressing question came from the Lord, **"But who do you say that I am?"**

Peter answered, **"You are the Christ, the Son of the living God."**

Jesus said to Peter, **"Blessed are you, Simon Bar-Jonah, for flesh and blood has not revealed this to you but My Father who is in heaven."** Matthew 16:13-17

There are so many we can follow in the footsteps of. So many voices out there that we can listen to such as political leaders, professors, teachers, pastors, a mentor, an ideal or philosophy but there is only One who has the words of eternal life. Whom are you following?

Sometimes the burdens get heavy Lord
And the clouds are closing in
But in my darkest hour I hear
Your tender voice whisper in my ear
Follow Me

Take My hand - I promise I will lead you
Trust in Me and believe - I'll never ever leave you
Follow Me

The road of life is not easy
Yet Jesus said, My burden is light
Daily you must count the cost
Deny yourself and pick up your own cross and
Follow Me

Take My hand - I promise I will lead you
Trust in Me and believe - I'll never ever leave you
Follow Me

Ever leave you - follow Me - take My hand
I promise I will lead you - trust in Me and believe
I'll never ever leave you - follow Me
Count the cost and follow Me

Praise to God my Father
For giving me Your Son
A love that is unending
Two hearts that beat as one
Nothing will ever separate
This bond I have with You
Eternal in the heavens
The only love that's true

Are You Ready?

I know they have been saying it
For many years
That Jesus Christ's return is very near
But never have the signs been so very clear
Jesus Christ is coming again
Are you ready?

They said it back in grandma's time
When she was just a child
And many now are skeptical
And choose to be defiled
But God is not a liar
That just is not His style
Jesus Christ is coming again
Are you ready?

Are you ready for His return
Does the fire within you burn
Remember Jesus paid the cost
The victory was His - Satan has lost
The battle was won - God's will was done

He's standing at the door of your heart
Are you ready?

2 Peter 3:9-10 tells us Jesus will come as a thief in the night and He is not slack concerning His promise but He is longsuffering toward us, not willing that any should perish but that all should come to repentance.
So don't be caught dead without Jesus.
Make sure you're ready!

Our Great God

"The pillars of heaven tremble, and are astonished at His rebuke. He stirs up the sea with His power, and by His understanding He breaks up the storm...But the thunder of His power who can understand?" **Job 26:11-12, 14**

When is the last time you watched the amazing show of a thunderstorm? The best fireworks from the Creator of the universe are put on display for all to see. The powerful bolts of visual electricity that light up the night sky as it strikes from the expanse of the highest part of the heavens to earth and the thunder that cracks like an explosion! All-powerful is our God!

God is all around us
If we'll just take the time
To look and see the splendor
That's right before our eyes
A newborn baby in our arms
Their tiny feet and hands
All speak to us of our great God
And His amazing plan
The beauty of a sunset
Painted all across the sky
The moon - the stars - the mighty sea
All creation testifies
Of our great God

Hold Fast to Jesus

There are times in all of our lives when we may be feeling worthless, anxious, depressed, or alone. The enemy of our soul feeds us lies especially in these vulnerable moments with such things as, "No one understands what you're going through and actually no one really cares. You are the only one in the world who is going through this hopeless situation. Your life means nothing. You really don't matter to anyone. If God really exists then where is He now?"

Lies! Lies! Lies! Speaking of the devil Jesus says in John 8:44, **"'…He was a murderer from the beginning, and does not stand in the truth, because there is no truth in him. When he speaks a lie, he speaks from his own resources, for he is a liar and the father of it.'"**

We must remember during our moments of despair that God has not forgotten us nor has He vacated His throne. His watchful eyes are upon every life on this earth and He knows **your** every thought and every detail of your life.
The following is personally for you.

Deep inside your heart
He sees your sorrows and fears
He sees the things no one else knows
Even the quiet, hidden tears
He knows you, dear child, beyond what you can comprehend
Remember that He has counted and knows
The very hairs of your head
He is your everything - He's all you could ever need
He sees your beauty among the thorns
Your longings - your desires
All of these He can meet

He knows your heart aches - He hears your every cry
Remember, His child, that He knows all
And it was for your life He died
He is your Creator - He knows what's best for you
He is sovereign - in control - yesterday, today, and forever, too
He sees your desire to be godly
So daily He's emptying more of you
To beautifully mold and shape you - to fill you afresh - anew
Just hold on, God's beautiful creation
He's engraved you on the palms of His hands
His watchful eye is upon you
Each day He unfolds for you His plan
Hold fast to Him for that time will come
When all pain and hurt will cease
For it is then that you will meet Him in glory and it will be
His face you see

Evelena (In the Twinkling of a Moment)

I still remember watching this frail elderly lady make her way down the center aisle at church on Sunday mornings to find her seat close to the front of the stage. She was dressed in her Sunday best. As the band began to lead the congregation in song I noticed her white gloved hands lifted high in worship to the One she loved. She was such an example to me in the short time that I knew her. When I heard she was in the hospital I went to visit her and she wasn't able to talk but I looked into her eyes and it was if I could see she was indicating that she was ready to depart to the waiting arms of her Savior. A few days later she went to her eternal home. What a joyous reunion it will soon be when we'll all be together again in the presence of our King and I will once again be able to see Evelena!

In the twinkling of a moment
In the blink of an eye
We will be together
To meet Him in the sky
What a joyous day that will be
When we're all together again
We'll never have to say goodbye
To family or to friends
Together with our Savior - We'll forever be
In the presence of the Father - For all eternity
Weeping may endure for a night
But joy comes in the morning
For I know that Evelena is satisfied
And with eagle's wings is soaring
In the Father's arms - Beholding the face
Of the One she loved so dear
Forever in the arms of Jesus
In the place of no more tears

What a blessing she has been to my life
And I'm sure to countless others
Beloved wife, beloved sister
Beloved friend, beloved mother
"Precious in the sight of the Lord
Is the death of one of His saints"
And truly this was Evelena's life
A masterpiece that only He could paint
Her life reflected the love of Christ
For all the world to see
Her life bore witness to His saving grace
Now in His presence forever she'll be
(And to Evelena's family) -
May you sense the presence of Jesus
The comfort and love that only He can bring
And with the dawning of each new day
May He give you a song to sing

In the Garden

In the garden where my Savior prayed,
Not My will but Yours - Oh Father God
May this cup pass away - Yet not My will but Yours
Thy will be done - for I am Your Son

All we like sheep have gone astray
Turned everyone to his own way
Take me to the garden - where I can pray
Thy will be done as it was for Your Son

In the garden where my Savior prayed
Shall I not pray there too?
Father God, the cup that Jesus drank - Shall I not drink it, too?
Thy will be done - as it was for Your Son
Let my will be Yours - This cup I shall endure

Here on the mountain beholding Your glory
I want to stay here forever and never return
To the valley below to the chaos of living
Because here on the mountain Your presence is known

But You have a purpose and You have a plan
I must take what I've learned and share it with man
And live with a passion for souls that are lost
To follow Your footsteps whatever the cost

I Am Yours

In my rejection and in my pain
I know You are with me
Though I'm alone and I am afraid
You're by my side
Though I don't feel You
Nor can I see You
I know that You love me
Because You said You'd never leave me
And You told me I am Your child
I am Yours
You are mine
Forever and ever
Until the clouds fade away
And the world is no more
I will see You
You will hold me forever and ever
Until that day - I will stay - close to Your heart

My Little Child

As I sat at my piano many years ago I was burdened over a certain individual in my life who was going through emotional distress, depression and feelings of rejection. I thought about what God would say to him. And the Lord reminded me that He is our Abba Father and we are His children, His sons and daughters. The following tender words came as I thought of the Lord God in our midst quieting His children with His love and rejoicing over us with singing. (**Zephaniah 3:17**)

My little child come unto Me
And give Me all your fears
The things that hurt that make you cry
And I'll bottle all your tears
Deeper than the ocean is My love for you
Nothing is impossible for Me to do

For I can't take My eyes off you
I love you, My little child
For I can't take My eyes off you
I love you, My little child
I love you

My Heart Longs for You

My heart longs for You
In a dry and thirsty land
My hope is in You
Oh God, I will yet praise You
I will worship You
Almighty God
Early will I seek You
To quiet my soul
Lifter of my head
Your beauty I behold
Source of living water
Come fill my thirsty soul
Oh Lord, fill my thirsty soul
My heart longs for You
In a dry and thirsty land
My hope is in You
Oh God, I will yet praise You
I will worship You
Almighty God
I will worship You
Almighty God

Mothers

One of the greatest callings that a woman can have upon her life is to be a mother. Though there is no financial gain involved and sometimes it is one of the most thankless jobs one could ever have it eventually reaps blessings that no amount of money could ever repay. To watch your children grow and become productive members of society and know that you were a help in that journey is worth every dirty diaper, every pile of laundry, every meal prepared, every school project worked on, every argument between siblings refereed, every teenage crisis, and so on... And to be the recipient of such a mother is a rich reward as well. The following "mom" poems were written with my precious mother in mind and as a mother myself, I hope that my kids would think the same of me -- knowing that I was a godly influence on them and that nothing done was in vain but all from a deep love for them.

For My Mom

Sometimes I take you for granted
Sometimes I don't show how I care
But deep inside the very soul of my heart
You're a treasure of beauty beyond compare

Patient and virtuous woman
A blessing from the Father above
His eyes behold His marvelous work
A masterpiece created for us to love

I love you with all of my heart
I love you, yes, I do

For what you've given me will last through eternity
A Mother's love

Forgive me for being ungrateful
For the times that I've caused you to cry
Thank you for your gentle quiet spirit
The love of Jesus I can see in your eyes
Someday I hope to have a family
And I pray I can somehow be
An example - an inspiration
The kind of mother you have been to me
I love you with all of my heart
I love you, yes, I do
For what you've given me will last through eternity
A Mother's love

Grateful

Grateful - I'm eternally grateful
For the love you've given me
Grateful - I'm eternally grateful
For the love you've given me
For the sleepless nights
As you'd wait for the morning light
For the sacrifices you've made for me
For the stories that you read
As you tucked me into bed
Making sure my prayers were always said
Grateful - I'm eternally grateful
For the love you've given me

Grateful - I'm eternally grateful
For the love you've given me
For those special needs
The broken hearts and wounded knees
For the kisses and the hugs you give so free
For the love you always share
To show me that you care
For giving up your job so you could be there
For me
Grateful - I'm eternally grateful
For the love you've given me
Grateful - I'm eternally grateful
For the love you've given me
And I'm thankful for that day
When you had me bow and pray
To ask Jesus in my heart and now I can say
Grateful - I'm eternally grateful
For the love you've given me
Grateful - I'm eternally grateful
For the love you've given me
You've given me

A Mother's Love

Caring for the family
Loving me day by day
Giving instead of taking
This has been your way
Patient and virtuous woman
For all the world to see
I am forever grateful
God gave you to me

*I have found in you
A friend forever
A love that is so strong
Binding us together
Forever - forever
A Mother's love*

*Teaching me from the Bible
Praying for my needs
Always understanding
Never judging me
No greater mom could I ask for
Someday I hope to be
An example and inspiration
Of what you've been to me
I have found in you
A friend forever
A love that is so strong
Binding us together
Forever - forever
A Mother's love*

A Beautiful Legacy

Reflecting on my mom's life I conclude that she truly was a beautiful soul. She was not famous and rich or highly educated with a Master's degree. She was not out working a full time job so that we could have more material possessions. She was not loud and pushy. She never raised her voice and degraded my dad or my siblings or me. She never obsessed about keeping a pristine home. She just wanted people to be comfortable. She was a good and kind woman who took care of her family. She simply did her best. Rarely would you know when she was in pain for she committed her suffering into the hands of the only One who could bring her comfort…even up to her last breath. The following was written with love in remembrance of her beautiful life.

One look into my Savior's eyes
He called out to my heart
Rise up My love, My fair one, it's time now to depart
Come with Me to heaven's home
Where peace and love abide
My child, My love, My fair one
My beautiful lovely bride
Come rest now from your labors
Lay down your weary soul
You're free from pain and sorrow
Enter into the joy of your Lord

I shall be satisfied as I live for Your glory, Lord
To love, to give, to bless
To speak Your word to a thirsty soul and
Truth to a world that needs Your rest

Keep the Fire Burning

Keep the fire burning in my heart and my soul
Live through me, Lord, live through me
Help me not to get discouraged by the enemy
Live through me, Lord, live through me

May Your light shine through the darkest moments of my life
Take me to the highest place where I can meet You
Face to face
Face to face
Oh, Lord

My Heart Belongs to You

You're my knight in shining armor
You're the answer to my dreams
You're everything I've hoped for
And everything I need
You are lovelier than diamonds
More desired than fine gold
You're the One that I've been waiting for
Your beauty I behold

My heart belongs to You - in Your presence I'll abide
I am Yours forever - You're my husband, I'm Your bride
All my life I've waited for this moment to arrive
Eternity together with my Lord Jesus Christ

You are fairer than the lilies
Brighter than the morning star
My Alpha and Omega the Shepherd of my heart
You're the blooming rose of Sharon
The beginning and the end - My Master and Creator
Forever my friend

Through the times ahead there'll be storms I must endure
Though this world will fail me
Your love is sure - ever sure

My heart belongs to You - in Your presence I'll abide
I am Yours forever - You're my husband I'm Your bride
All my life I've waited for this moment to arrive
Eternity together with my Lord Jesus Christ

His Message Is Simple

His message is simple
But yet so divine
Accept Him today
You haven't much time

He came once to earth
With a meek and kind heart
He died for our sins
And then did depart

He arose from the dead
After being crucified on a cross
He ascended to Heaven
As He paid the highest cost

He came once as a Savior
And He's coming back again
Of the time no one knows
Not even the angels know when

But He's definitely coming
To judge all great and small
This message to you
Could be His last call

This world can't go on
With the mess that it's in
It's time to confess the name of Jesus
He will forgive all your sins

Christ is the good Shepherd
His sheep hear His voice
It's all up to you now
Only you can make the choice

I Love You

You're the love of my life
You're the reason I live
Every beat of my heart
Belongs to You
My life is in Your hands
I'm entrusted to Your plan
No greater love
Have I ever known

You are everything to me
Everything I've hoped for
Everything I need
And I give my heart and soul to You
Because You are - my true love

Other loves have come and gone
But You're the One that's true
Everlasting - without end
I love You

Whom Have I in Heaven but You
(Psalm 73:25, 84:2)

Whom have I in heaven but You
Whom have I
Whom have I in heaven but You
Whom have I
My heart and flesh cry out for You
For the living God
For You are great and wonderful
Oh, Most High
Whom have I in heaven but You
Whom have I
Whom have I in heaven but You
Whom have I

What a Wonderful God

Whom shall I fear, Lord, when You are my light
Guiding my way, Lord, through the day and night
Always surrounding my life with Your love
What wondrous light
What wondrous love
What a wonderful God

Darkness shall flee, Lord, when You are near
My life's in Your hands, I've nothing to fear
When troubles surround me - I call out Your name
What wondrous light
What wondrous love
What a wonderful God

Not by Might

Not by might - Nor by power
But by My Spirit says the Lord
May He be your source of comfort
As you weather through this storm
When your heart is overwhelmed
And your pillow is drenched with tears
When the night is full of shadows
Know that morning is very near
The sun will rise upon another day
And God's presence will greet you again
His arms waiting to hold you close
And to be your ever present friend
What comfort to know He understands your pain
He hears your cries and His love remains
May you cling to your faith
May you stand on God's Word
Keep your eyes fixed on Jesus
Toward heaven - our eternal home
His love has no bounds or limits
His favor is for life
Weeping may endure for a night
But joy comes with the morning light

You Are Worthy of My Complete Devotion

You are worthy of my complete devotion
For there is no one like You
I was lost until You found me
You captured my heart
No one has loved me as You do

Every hurt, every tear
Every need, every fear
Every day, every night
In the dark or the light
You are there

You are the One who holds my hand
You carry me - You understand
Every thought, every care
You even account for all my hair
What an awesome God You are
In humility I bow before You now

A Gift Cannot Be Measured

For my daughter's wedding I had been asked to describe what the groom would be getting in marrying my daughter and I was to read it to him during the ceremony. I prayed for the Lord to direct me and this is what He had me share...

A gift cannot be measured by the wrapping and the bows
It's what's inside that matters - it's where the beauty grows
Tiffany is a precious gift - A blessing from the Lord
On loan to us for such a short time - Now He's given her to become yours
She's a lady and a princess
For she's the daughter of the King
The Lord of all creation who gave His everything
Her heart belongs to Jesus - He's the Savior of her soul
Her sins are all forgiven
Because His blood has made her whole
She's a precious gift from heaven - The apple of God's eye
She's been her daddy's little girl
And her mommy's joy and pride
Her worth is far above rubies - More valuable than gold
A spring shut up - a fountain sealed - a garden enclosed
Standing here before you now is the beautiful bride of Christ
The symbol of God's holy church - His glory and His pride
And you, as the bridegroom, are a symbol
Of our Jesus Christ
Who gave Himself in sacrifice - For <u>His</u> beloved bride
So treasure this - your precious gift - For I can surely see
That Jesus truly loves you, Joel - For He's given you Tiffany

Great is the Lord and worthy to be praised
He alone is God
He is your strength when you are weak
He is your comfort when you are in pain
He is always near
He will answer when you call
He never changes
He is constant, He is kind
He is Lord over all creation
He will never leave you or forsake you
He is Father, He is friend
He is husband
He is the lover of your soul
He is all knowing, everlasting
He is God

When I Count My Blessings

When I count my blessings
I think of you
For your friendship
Your fellowship
For all that you do
There's a special place within my heart
Reserved just for you
For when I count my blessings
I think of you

Plant These Seeds

Are you feeling down? Perhaps you're depressed. Having a "woe is me" pity party? Are you feeling as if you're the only one who is going through it? Well, you're not! Everyone faces life's "blues" at one time or another and some more than others. But there is a cure for this. How about a challenge to help change your outlook by getting your eyes off yourself and turning them to others in need? A simple suggestion: try doing something random and kind for someone. Look around, there are countless people who need "cheering up" right now. So, allow the Lord to use your life to bless someone. Your act of kindness doesn't have to be huge or sensational or cost a lot of money and it doesn't need to take up a lot of your time. Think of it as planting seeds in the garden of life.

I saw my next door neighbor as I walked along the way
She asked me why such sadness filled my tired face
She handed me a bag with a note she said to read
And told me it should make me smile and be all that I need
I'll never forget the kindness she showed me on that day
It left a lasting imprint and eased my inner pain
Inside the bag she gave me
were some seeds and a detailed note
The following is what it said, this is what she wrote:

Plant these seeds when you get home
Give them water and watch them grow
In your garden or in a pot
Just remember to plant these Forget-Me-Nots
And when you see the flowers bud
May it remind you of all God's done
Each bloom a blessing for you to receive
His countless wonders for you - for me
And may the seeds you sow today

Be ones of kindness along the way
The seeds of goodness
The seeds of love
Watered by the Father above
Each little act of mercy
Each little act of grace
Will never go unnoticed
When done in Jesus' name
So grow where you are planted
In the garden of this life
May you be a sweet aroma
A living sacrifice

Just for Today

Just for today - I will trust in You Jesus
Just for today - I'll serve You Lord
Just for today - I'll walk in Your footsteps
Seeking You more and more
Just this moment in time is what You've given me
I will not look back - for yesterday is gone
I can't change what is already over
So for today in Your strength I'll carry on
I must remember tomorrow is not guaranteed
For all of life is in Your very hands
Help me live for today and not waste it
For tomorrow - today will be gone

The Lamb Who Died for Me

At times it gets cold here in the shadows
To never be used as I desire
I'll be content while others shine - if that's Your will
I'll even stay a step behind
As long as You get all of the glory
I'll patiently wait for You to work
Down on my knees I'll pray to You - forever
I'll praise You for all that You do

I want You to know I love You, Jesus
You're everything I will ever need
Someday I'll sing with all the angels
For You are the Lamb who died for me

Sometimes it appears I seem ungrateful
While You have all things under control
You are the Potter, I'm the clay - You're Jehovah
And in my life please have Your way

I want You to know I love You, Jesus
You're everything I will ever need
Someday I'll sing with all the angels
For You are the Lamb who died for me

Oh, the Lamb who died for me - You, You, You
You are the Lamb who died for me
Praise, praise, I'll praise You all my days
I'll praise You in every way
Thank You, thank You, thank God for You
The Lamb who died for me

At the Cross

At the cross
I lay my burdens down
And I seek the One I love
Who bore my shame
All my guilt and sin
Who died and rose again
And I see You now
As the blood flows down
From the crown of thorns
Pressed on Your brow
I see Your arms stretched wide
As they pierced Your side
I see the love within Your eyes
At the cross

The Image of God

"But we all, with unveiled face, beholding as in a mirror the glory of the Lord, are being transformed into the same image from glory to glory, just as by the Spirit of the Lord."
2 Corinthians 3:18

Man was originally created in the image of God. (Genesis 1:26). If Eve and Adam had not sinned they would have lived forever. Think of it -- they would have been ageless and never died; thus, it would have been for all mankind. But as we know they did disobey God and the fall of man brought sin and death to all who entered the world since then. The perfect image was distorted. It is God's desire and purpose to restore us back into His image as we look at the glory of Jesus. As we read His word, put into action what He says, and allow Him to change us from within others will see His likeness in us. We can be mirrors that brightly reflect His glory. We will never attain perfection on this side of Heaven but we can reflect more of Jesus to a world that desperately needs to see Him in action through our transformed lives. To see His unconditional love, grace, mercy, kindness, forgiveness, humility, selflessness.
What do you see when you look in the mirror?

When I look in the mirror I see the wrinkles of age
Yet as I grow older I need to see the miracle of grace
The transforming power of the Spirit of the Lord
Is restoring me to my original form
To be more and more like Jesus shall be my story
Of the image in the mirror reflecting His glory
Use me to spread Your Word like a sweet perfume
A fragrance that diffuses into every room
In the hearts and the minds of every soul that I meet
May You, oh Jesus, be all that they see

Higher Ground

Growing up is not so easy
Pressures face me all around
Hold me tight, Lord, when I'm falling
Take me to that higher ground

When I'm with You I feel comfort
In Your arms I am secure
Guard my steps, Lord, lead me onward
Pleasing You with a life that's pure - and take me to

Higher ground
Above the confusion that surrounds me
Higher ground
To that place where peace is found
Higher ground - only in You - is higher ground

Don't be fooled by the illusions
See the picture - it is clear
Life is better if you'll listen
To the Spirit's voice in your ear
And take me to

Higher ground
Above the confusion that surrounds me
Higher ground
To that place where peace is found
Higher ground - only in You - is higher ground

My Heart Longs for Heaven

"'Let not your heart be troubled; you believe in God, believe also in Me. In My Father's house are many mansions; if it were not so, I would have told you. I go to prepare a place for you. And if I go and prepare a place for you, I will come again and receive you to Myself; that where I am, there you may be also. And where I go you know, and the way you know.'" John 14:1-4

What precious words of promise from Jesus. He knew what His followers were about to face. They were going to see their Teacher and Friend mocked by those He walked among, beaten beyond recognition, humiliated, crucified on a cross and put into a grave. But Jesus knew that death was not the end for Him for on the third day He would rise and appear to them in the days afterward. Therefore He tells them to not be troubled, worried, distressed. His destination was Heaven and He said He was going there to make ready a room for each of them in His Father's house and they would be with Him once again forever.

The disciples would live on and face much hardship and persecution for their faith but the promise from their Lord in this passage would be in their memory to hold on to until the end of their days.

This promise is for us, too. No one needs to feel lost in this world when Jesus is the way to get home. Oh, how our hearts should long for Heaven!

My heart longs for Heaven - where You are
It's a place that I know of - way beyond the stars
My heart longs for Heaven - free at last

No more tears, pain, or sorrow all that is in the past
Someday I'll see You face to face
I'll wake up with Your warm embrace around me
You'll bring me home to Paradise
Away above the clouds that rise
That's where You'll take me
My heart longs for Heaven - come, my Lord
Take Your bride to be with You - now and forevermore
I'm longing for the day I'll be - with You, my King
For all eternity

You Are Altogether Lovely

I am filled with a sense of Your beauty
Your greatness, Your goodness, Your love
And deep within the very soul of my heart
I long to be forever Yours
You are altogether lovely
Everything I've been searching for
And with each new day that passes
I grow to love You more
You are altogether lovely
Everything I've been searching for
And with each new day that passes
I grow to love You more
Keep me forever Yours

America so Beautiful

***"Righteousness exalts a nation, but sin is a reproach to any people."* Proverbs 14:34**

Land of the free and home of the brave
Names we have been called
America so beautiful
How great will be your fall
This nation founded under God
No longer seeks His face
Doing what's right in one's own eyes
We have fallen from His grace
Drive by shootings - gangs and drugs
Abortion on the rise
No sanctity of marriage
No thought to take one's life
Your founding fathers, America
Fought to win this land
They gave their lives in sacrifice
To fulfill God's perfect plan
We must return to the living God
To keep our country free
He's the only hope we have today
May He shed His grace on thee

America, Where Is Your God?

Founded on the faith of our fathers
A nation standing upon God's Word
What happened to the morals of our people
As in generations gone on before
America, Where is Your God
America, land that I love
The God who made us free
And gave us liberty
Where is He now, America?

"If My people who are called by My Name will humble themselves and pray and seek My face and turn from their wicked ways then I will hear from Heaven and will forgive their sin and heal their land." (2 Chronicles 7:14)

America, please hear your God
America, land that He loves
The God who made us free
Is calling you and me
Please hear Him now, America
Please hear Him now, America

There's Just Something about Christmas

It seems as the summer ends and the weather turns a bit cooler and the stores begin to put hints of Christmas decorations on their shelves that something joyous is stirred within and the thought of the Christmas season approaching creates an inner excitement that no other season quite brings. The sights, the smells, the holiday fragrances, the gathering of family and friends, the decorating and the lights, the plays and choirs singing -- all add to the anticipation of the coming celebration. But before we allow ourselves to get caught up in all the hustle and bustle -- the true reality of every believer is the remembrance of a Savior born one holy night in Bethlehem who came to set the world free from sin and darkness. Jesus is our one true focus to not lose sight of at this special time of year.

Oh come let us adore Him - Let all creation sing
The Son of God came to this world
To pardon all man's sin
He alone is worthy - The Name above all names
Let every heart, Let every knee bow down and give Him praise
Emmanuel - God with us
All glory to Jesus our King
From birth to death - He gave it all
Humble Lamb of offering
Hallelujah - Hallelujah
As heaven and nature proclaim
That Jesus is Lord and He has been born
Into every heart of man
Open the eyes of the blind that they may behold their God
The King of all creation has come to dwell with us
His Name is Wonderful, Counselor, Mighty God,
Prince of Peace
He is everything we'll ever want - And all we'll ever need

Unwrap the Gift

Love came down on Christmas day
Wrapped in flesh - His Life He gave
The greatest gift the world has known
God sent His Son from Heaven's throne

Unwrap the gift - it's free
The Father bids to come receive
And in your heart believe
He paid the price for you and me

One holy night in Bethlehem
The Lamb of God - The Great I AM
Delivered to a world in need
God's only Son for you and me

Unwrap the gift - it's free
The Father bids to come receive
And in your heart believe
He paid the price for you and me

Unwrap the gift - it's free
The Father bids to come receive
And in your heart believe
He paid the price for you and me

My Christmas Prayer for You

Deny yourself, take up your cross, and learn to follow Me
These are the words of Jesus to all who will receive
He never promised riches or fame of any kind
The way is very narrow which very few will find
There will be trials and temptations and pain along the way
Yet through these times of suffering we fervently will pray
And just like our Lord and Savior we desire more to be
A servant of our God and King whose glory soon we'll see
He said His yoke is easy and His burden - it is light
There's nothing that's impossible for our God
Who dwells on high
Our Redeemer, Friend, and Counselor
The Prince of Peace is He
The First and Last, the God of hope, forever He will be
The precious Lamb Who sacrificed His very life for us
And all He asks of you and me is to walk by faith and trust
Let's reflect upon this time of year
When we celebrate Christ's birth
When God came down in human flesh to live upon this earth
From a Baby in a manger to a Man upon a cross
He laid aside His royalty and counted it but loss
His wondrous love has no bounds - it heals the broken heart
It mends a wounded spirit and gives a brand new start
It flows on like a river into an ocean wide
And melts away the cancerous sin
That has plagued us deep inside

The only thing that matters as Christmas day draws near
Is where does your heart's treasure lie
Is it in Heaven or is it here?
Immanuel - God with us has come to set us free
Choose life today and live for Christ who offers eternity.
The greatest gift the world could know or ever could receive
Was wrapped in love one blessed night
Unwrap it and believe.
This is my Christmas prayer for you
That you will know God's Son
And grow in grace and knowledge of this Wondrous Holy One

A Christmas Letter

Dear family and friends as Christmas draws near
From my heart to yours I send my love
And want to express great gratitude to you
For my life has been deeply touched
Each person - each life - that has come my way
Some passing by quickly and some having stayed
Yet you each have made an imprint forever forged
In my mind and heart - How I thank the Lord!
Your smiles - your laughter - your love - your prayers
The ways you've shown that you truly care
The cards - the texts - the phone calls - the letters
With words to encourage "that things will get better"
May you know that you're loved way beyond measure
And that to God and me you are a priceless treasure
No gift could replace the things that you've done
Yes, I am forever grateful to Jesus, God's Son
My life would be meaningless had you not been a part
These things that I'm writing come straight from my heart
For Christmas is a time to reflect on what's true
That Jesus has been born for me and you
It's a time to give and a time to receive
A time to share what we truly believe
So from my heart to yours upon this holy day
*May you know that **you** are special in every way*
Your gifts - your talents - the things done out of love
Do not go unnoticed by the lives that you've touched
May your Christmas be filled with the beauty of Christ
And may you continue to touch others with your life

Emmanuel Has Come

On the day that You were born
All the earth bowed down
The rocks cried out - the angels sang
As the shepherds gathered round
Mary pondered in her heart
This blessing in her arms
She knew the eyes she gazed into
Were the very eyes of God - Were the very eyes of God

Rejoice - rejoice - Emmanuel
Has come for you and come for me
Has come to Israel

On this day this Christmas morn
Let the earth bow down
Our hearts cry out - the choirs sing
As Your people gather round
Let us ponder in our hearts
This blessing born today
And may we know this love we feel
Is the love that died to save - Is the love that died to save

Rejoice - rejoice - Emmanuel
Has come for you and come for me
Has come to Israel
Into our hearts to dwell - Our King Emmanuel

Christmas Message

A message from my heart to yours upon this Christmas Eve
May you and yours be blessed this day
And in your souls believe
That Jesus is our Savior and ever guiding light
He's the Alpha and Omega our keeper in the night
His life He held in no regard when from His Father's side
He left the beauty of heaven to come to us and abide
From an infant little baby to a child and then a man
He knows our every weakness, our thoughts, and all our plans
He knows our feelings big and small - He's felt our every pain
He's been there through the good and bad
The heartache and the shame
He's walked the path before us
There's nothing He can't do
He's the God of all creation - forever faithful and true
He paid a debt we could not pay as God's sacrificial Lamb
The thorns, the stripes, the nails and scars upon the
Great I AM
He did it all for you and me and He'd do it all again
His love is so amazing - I can barely comprehend
Stand in awe of the King of kings - He's worthy to be praised
Let's worship Him with thankful hearts each and every day
My prayer for you this Christmas is to be closer to our Lord
And in the days that lie ahead to be of one accord
Serving Him with all your heart - in love and unity
Until the day He takes us home where forever we'll be free

He'll Meet You Here

The prophet Joel writes in Joel 3:14, **"Multitudes, multitudes in the valley of decision! For the day of the Lord is near in the valley of decision."**

Every day we are faced with decisions. Some decisions are no-brainers such as what will I wear or what will I eat. Should I comb my hair, take a shower, brush my teeth?
But there are certain decisions that are life-changing if we choose without much thought or prayer. Will I go to school or drop out? Will I try alcohol or cigarettes or drugs? Will I let my eyes wander to that questionable website on the internet? Should I marry this person even though I sense hesitation? What schooling do I need for that career?
It is true that the decisions we make today will affect our tomorrows. And with that thought in mind the most important decision any human being on planet earth will ever make is where will I spend eternity?
The statistics are staggering. One out of every person will die. We are not going to be living here forever. Death is no respecter of a person's age. It's not just the elderly that pass on. Babies, teenagers, those in their 20s, 30s, 40s, 50s -- all die -- male or female, rich or poor, the educated, the Christian, the Jew, the Muslim, the atheist. All will breathe their last, and then????
The question remains and there is an answer. God!
God is real. Look around. All that you see did not just poof or evolve. Every creation must have a creator! Think of a beautiful painting, sculpture, or amazing structures such as the Empire State Building or the Taj Mahal. Should we be so silly to think that they just appeared out of nowhere? They had to have a designer/creator!
So who created the world?

The Master Designer, God, created the world and all that is in it. Mankind rebelled against Holy God and thus our sins separated us from Him. God came down to earth in the form of a man, the Man Christ Jesus, to die for all mankind's sin and He rose the third day overcoming death and the grave. Do you know anyone willing to die for you?

"You see, at just the right time, when we were still powerless, Christ died for the ungodly. Very rarely will anyone die for a righteous person, though for a good person someone might possibly dare to die. But God demonstrates his own love for us in this: While we were still sinners, Christ died for us." Romans 5:6-8 NIV

Today is the day. If you are feeling a tug on your heart don't ignore the Spirit of God as He is drawing you to Himself. Don't wait to make the **most important decision** of your life. Do it now!
It's as simple as this, "Jesus, I confess to You that I am a sinner and I accept You as my Savior. I believe You died and rose and that You are God."
He waits for you...

Can you see Him - He's standing here
With arms wide open to draw you near
He bids you come now just as you are
His love is reaching into your heart

And I beg you by the mercies of God
If you hear Him won't you come to the cross
Lay down your burdens
You need not fear
Jesus is waiting
He'll meet you here
Jesus is waiting
He'll meet you here

Made in the USA
Columbia, SC
04 January 2025